A New Tuna

Experience

Amazing Tuna Recipes You Will

Absolutely Love

By

Heston Brown

HESTON BROWN

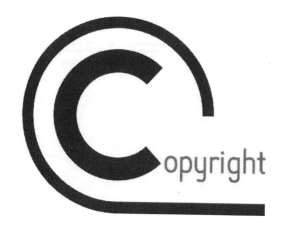

Copyright 2019 Heston Brown

Thank you so much for buying my book! I want to give you a special gift!

Receive a special gift as a thank you for buying my book. Now you will be able to benefit from free and discounted book offers that are sent directly to your inbox every week.

To subscribe simply fill in the box below with your details and start reaping the rewards! A new deal will arrive every day and reminders will be sent so you never miss out. Fill in the box below to subscribe and get started!

https://heston-brown.getresponsepages.com

Subscribe to our newsletter

Your Email   >

Table of Contents

Chapter I - Delicious and Colored Tuna Salad Recipes

Our culinary trip continues with some colored, textured and very flavored tuna salads. Discover and enjoy them!

XXXXXXXXXXXXXXXXXXXXXXXXXXXXXXXXXXXXX

Recipe 1: Tuna and Bread Salad

Try this for lunch and you will feel great all day!

Prep Time: 10 minutes

Total Prep Time: 10 minutes

Serving Sizes:4

List of Ingredients:

- 1 cup canned white beans, drained
- 1 cup cherry tomatoes cut in halves
- Salt and black pepper to the taste
- 1 shallot thinly sliced
- 6 ounces canned tuna, drained
- 2 tsp. mustard
- ½ baguette cut in cubes
- 1 Tbsp. balsamic vinegar
- ¼ cup kalamata olives, pitted
- 2 Tbsp. basil chopped
- 3 Tbsp. extra virgin olive oil

xxxxxxxxxxxxxxxxxxxxxxxxxxxxxxxxxxxxxxxxx

Instructions:

1. In a bowl, mix tomatoes with salt and pepper to the taste and leave aside for 10 minutes.

2. Add tuna, beans, shallots and olives and toss to coat.

3. Add bread cubes and toss to coat again.

4 In another bowl, mix vinegar with mustard, salt and pepper to the taste and stir well.

5. Add oil and basil and stir again well.

6. Pour this over salad, stir gently and serve right away.

Enjoy!

Recipe 2: The Best Tuna and Potato Salad

It's a fresh, spring salad! Try it now!

Prep Time: 10 minutes

Total Prep Time: 25 minutes

Serving Sizes:4

List of Ingredients:

- 12 ounces new potatoes
- 4 Tbsp. homemade mayonnaise
- 4 anchovy fillets
- Juice from 1 lemon
- A bunch spring onions chopped
- 1 lettuce, leaves torn
- 12 ounces canned tuna steak in oil
- Black pepper to the taste

xxxxxxxxxxxxxxxxxxxxxxxxxxxxxxxxxxxxxxxxx

Instructions:

1. Put water in a pot, add potatoes, place on stove, bring to a boil over medium heat, boil for 15 minutes, drain, rinse with cold water, slice and put in a salad bowl.

2. In a small bowl, mix mayo with anchovies, lemon juice and black pepper to the taste and stir very well.

3. Add lettuce leaves and tuna to potatoes and stir gently.

4. Add salad dressing, toss to coat and serve right away.

Enjoy!

Recipe 3: Tuna and White Beans Salad

Try it right away!

Prep Time: 10 minutes

Total Prep Time: 10 minutes

Serving Sizes:4

List of Ingredients:

- 12 ounces canned dark tuna, flaked and oil from the can reserved
- 30 ounces canned cannellini white beans, drained
- 1/3 cup capers, drained
- 6 Tbsp. red wine vinegar
- Salt and black pepper to the taste
- 1 red onion thinly sliced
- 1 and ½ cups cherry tomatoes
- 6 basil leaves, torn
- 2 cups arugula

XXXXXXXXXXXXXXXXXXXXXXXXXXXXXXXXXXXXXXXX

Instructions:

1. In a bowl, mix tuna with beans and capers and toss to coat.

2. Put reserved oil in another bowl, add vinegar, salt and pepper to the taste and stir very well.

3. Pour this over tuna and beans and toss to coat.

4. Add tomatoes and red onions and toss again.

5. Arrange arugula on a platter, add tuna salad on top and garnish with basil.

Enjoy!

Recipe 4: Wonderful Tuna and Carrot Salad

We just love this salad! It's because it is so tasty!

Prep Time: 5 minutes

Total Prep Time: 15 minutes

Serving Sizes:4

List of Ingredients:

- ¼ yellow onion finely chopped
- 4 carrots cut in thin matchsticks
- 1 Tbsp. extra-virgin olive oil
- 1 garlic clove finely chopped
- 6 ounces canned white tuna, drained and flaked
- 1 Tbsp. mustard
- 1 Tbsp. red wine vinegar
- Salt and black pepper to the taste
- 1 Tbsp. lemon juice

XXXXXXXXXXXXXXXXXXXXXXXXXXXXXXXXXXXXXXXXX

Instructions:

1. In a bowl, mix vinegar with salt, pepper, mustard and lemon juice, stir very well and leave aside.

2. Heat up a pan with the oil over medium heat, add onion and cook for 5 minutes stirring often.

3. Add garlic, stir and cook 1 more minute.

4. Add carrots, stir and cook for another 5 minutes.

5. Take off heat, leave aside to cool down and transfer to a salad bowl.

6. Add tuna and the salad dressing, toss to coat and keep in the fridge until you serve it.

Enjoy!

Recipe 5: Great Tuna and Couscous Salad

It's an Israeli style salad that tastes great!

Prep Time: 5 minutes

Total Prep Time: 35 minutes

Serving Sizes:8

List of Ingredients:

- 12 ounces couscous
- 14 ounces canned tuna, drained and flaked
- ¼ cup lemon juice
- Grated zest from 2 lemons
- 3 Tbsp. capers, drained
- ½ cup extra virgin olive oil
- ½ cup black olives, pitted and chopped
- ½ cup red peppers, roasted, jarred and diced
- Salt and black pepper to the taste
- 4 cups water
- 2 tsp. garlic finely minced
- ¼ cup basil roughly chopped
- 1 cup scallions finely chopped
- Juice from ½ lemon

XXXXXXXXXXXXXXXXXXXXXXXXXXXXXXXXXXXXXXXXXX

Instructions:

1. Put 4 cups water in a pot, bring to a boil over medium heat, add couscous, reduce heat to low, cover pot, simmer for 15 minutes, drain and transfer to a bowl.

2. In a bowl, mix tuna with lemon juice, ¼ cup olive oil, lemon zest, olives, peppers, capers, garlic, salt and black pepper to the taste and stir.

3. Add couscous, cover bowl and leave aside for 15 minutes, stirring from time to time.

4. When the time has passed, add scallions and basil and juice from ½ lemon, toss to coat and serve.

Enjoy!

Recipe 6: Healthy Tuna Salad

Try this Mediterranean style salad as soon as possible!

Prep Time: 10 minutes

Total Prep Time: 10 minutes

Serving Sizes:4

List of Ingredients:

- 1 baby lettuce, leaves torn
- 1 cucumber cubed
- 1 red onion thinly sliced
- 7 ounces red grape tomatoes cut in halves
- 1 green capsicum cubed
- Salt and black pepper to the taste
- 2/3 cup feta cheese, shredded
- 2 Tbsp. oregano finely chopped
- 2/3 cup kalamata olives, pitted and chopped
- ¼ cup red wine vinegar
- 13 ounces canned tuna, undrained and flaked
- Bread slices, toasted for serving

Instructions:

1. In a bowl, mix lettuce with cucumber, onions, tomatoes, capsicum, oregano and olives,

2. Add tuna, cheese, salt and pepper to the taste, drizzle vinegar at the end and toss to coat.

3. Serve with toasted bread slices.

Enjoy!

Recipe 7: Amazing Tuna Salad

It's amazing and delicious! What more can you want?

Prep Time: 10 minutes

Total Prep Time: 10 minutes

Serving Sizes: 2

List of Ingredients:

- 8 ounces canned tuna, flaked, packed in olive oil, oil reserved
- 2 Tbsp. shallot finely chopped
- 4 butter lettuce leaves
- 1 Tbsp. capers, drained
- 2 Tbsp. red bell pepper chopped
- 1 Tbsp. micro greens
- 2 Tbsp. hardboiled egg, chopped
- Salt and black pepper to the taste
- Juice from ½ lemon

XXXXXXXXXXXXXXXXXXXXXXXXXXXXXXXXXXXXXXXX

Instructions:

1. Put tuna in a bowl and introduce in the fridge for a few minutes.

2. Divide lettuce leaves on plates, add tuna, shallot, capers, bell pepper, micro greens and egg.

3. Add salt and pepper to the taste and toss to coat.

4. Add reserved oil from tuna and lemon juice, toss to coat again and serve right away!

Enjoy!

Chapter II - Special Tuna Recipes for Breakfast

Begin your beautiful day with some of the best tuna recipes for breakfast! Try them all and be amazed!

xxxxxxxxxxxxxxxxxxxxxxxxxxxxxxxxxxxxxxxx

Recipe 8: Delicious Tuna Frittata

Try this breakfast frittata right away!

Prep Time: 5 minutes

Total Prep Time: 20 minutes

Serving Sizes:4

List of Ingredients:

- 10 ounces canned tuna
- 5 eggs whisked
- ½ cup favorite cheese shredded
- Salt and black pepper to the taste
- 3 tsp. cooking oil

XXXXXXXXXXXXXXXXXXXXXXXXXXXXXXXXXXXXXXXXXX

Instructions:

1. Grease a pie dish with the cooking oil and leave aside for now.

2. In a bowl, mix tuna with eggs, salt and pepper to the taste and stir very well.

3. Pour this into dish, introduce in the oven at 370 degrees F and bake for 14 minutes.

4. Sprinkle shredded cheese on top, introduce in the oven for 3-4 more minutes, cut and divide on plates and serve.

Enjoy!

Recipe 9: Tuna and Avocado Breakfast Tostadas

It has such an amazing taste!

Prep Time: 5 minutes

Total Prep Time: 15 minutes

Serving Sizes:4

List of Ingredients:

- 1 avocado, mashed
- 1 Tbsp. red onion finely chopped
- 4 ounces canned tuna, drained
- Salt and black pepper to the taste
- 1 Tbsp. scallion finely chopped
- 4 slices whole wheat bread
- 1 Tbsp. lime juice

xxxxxxxxxxxxxxxxxxxxxxxxxxxxxxxxxxxxxxx

Instructions:

1. Arrange bread slices on a baking sheet, introduce in the oven at 400 degrees F, bake for 5 minutes, take them out of the oven and leave them aside for now.

2. In a bowl, mix tuna with mashed avocado and stir well.

3. Add salt and black pepper to the taste, lime juice, scallions and onion and stir well again.

4. Spread 3 Tbsp. tuna mix on each bread slice, sprinkle some red onion on top of each and serve.

Enjoy!

Recipe 10: Tuna and Egg Sandwich

Eat this for breakfast and you won't feel hungry all day!

Prep Time: 10 minutes

Total Prep Time: 30 minutes

Serving Sizes:2

List of Ingredients:

- 2 Tbsp. green onion finely diced
- ¼ red bell pepper chopped
- 1 tsp. coconut oil
- 1 egg
- 2 egg whites
- Salt and black pepper to the taste
- ½ tsp. turmeric
- 5 ounces canned tuna, drained
- 4 slices bread
- 3 Tbsp. canned green chilies chopped
- 2 tomato slices
- Sriracha sauce for serving

xxxxxxxxxxxxxxxxxxxxxxxxxxxxxxxxxxxxxxxx

Instructions:

1. Heat up a pan with the coconut oil over medium heat, add bell pepper and onions, stir and cook for 7 minutes.

2. In a bowl, mix egg with egg whites, salt, pepper and turmeric and whisk well.

3. Add this to the pan and cook for 3 minutes stirring all the time.

4. Add chilies and tuna, stir and cook for 3 more minutes.

5. Toast your bread and arrange slices on a plate.

6. Take tuna scrambled eggs off heat, divide on 2 slices of bread, add a tomato slice on each and Sriracha sauce and top with the other 2 slices of bread.

7. Serve right away!

Enjoy!

Recipe 11: Tasty Tuna and Spinach Sandwich

You will fill full all day with this tasty and nutritious sandwich!

Prep Time: 5 minutes

Total Prep Time: 5 minutes

Serving Sizes: 2

List of Ingredients:

- 6 ounces canned tuna, drained
- 4 slices whole wheat bread
- 1 Tbsp. homemade mayo
- A handful baby spinach
- Salt and black pepper to the taste
- Some cheese spread
- A splash of white wine vinegar

xxxxxxxxxxxxxxxxxxxxxxxxxxxxxxxxxxxxxxx

Instructions:

1. In a bowl, mix tuna with mayo and stir well.

2. Add salt, pepper to the taste and a splash of vinegar and stir well again.

3. Spread cheese spread on 2 bread slices, add tuna and mayo mix and spread, top with baby spinach leaves and then with the other slices of bread.

4. Cut each sandwich in half, arrange on plates and serve.

Enjoy!

Recipe 12: Breakfast Tuna Omelette

Make this omelette for breakfast tomorrow and your family with definitely appreciate it!

Prep Time: 10 minutes

Total Prep Time: 15 minutes

Serving Sizes: 2

List of Ingredients:

- 6 ounces canned tuna, drained
- A pinch of coriander
- A pinch of paprika
- 3 eggs
- ¼ cup low fat milk
- Salt and black pepper to the taste
- 1 tomato thinly sliced
- 3 spring onions thinly sliced
- 2 Tbsp. parsley finely chopped

XXXXXXXXXXXXXXXXXXXXXXXXXXXXXXXXXXXXXXX

Instructions:

1. In a bowl, mix eggs with coriander, paprika, milk, salt and black pepper to the taste and whisk well.

2. Add spring onions and stir again.

3. Spray some cooking oil in a pan, heat up over medium high heat, add egg mix, cook without stirring for 2-3 minutes, arrange tomato slices on one half, add tuna on top, flip the other side of the omelette and fold over tuna and tomato, cook for another 2 minutes and take off heat.

4. Divine on 2 plates, sprinkle parsley on top and serve.

Enjoy!

Recipe 13: Breakfast Tuna Quesadilla

We really recommend you try this quick breakfast quesadilla!

Prep Time: 10 minutes

Total Prep Time: 20 minutes

Serving Sizes:3

List of Ingredients:

- ¼ cup homemade mayonnaise
- 12 ounces canned tuna, drained and flaked
- 6 flour tortillas
- ¼ cup already made salsa
- ¾ cup cheddar cheese, shredded
- Cooking spray

XXXXXXXXXXXXXXXXXXXXXXXXXXXXXXXXXXXXXXXXX

Instructions:

1. In a bowl, mix salsa with tuna and mayo and stir well.

2. Spread this on half of the tortillas, sprinkle cheese all over, cover them with the rest of the tortillas and put on a plate.

3. Spray some cooking oil in a pan, heat up over medium high heat, add quesadillas, cook until they brown, flip and cook until they brown on this side as well, transfer to a plate and serve right away.

Enjoy!

Recipe 14: Healthy Tuna Breakfast

It's an easy recipe but extremely healthy one at the same time!

Prep Time: 10 minutes

Total Prep Time: 12 minutes

Serving Sizes: 2

List of Ingredients:

- 1 whole wheat English muffin cut in halves
- 6 ounces canned tuna, drained and flaked
- 2 Tbsp. tomato sauce
- Salt and black pepper to the taste
- A pinch of dried oregano
- 2 slices mozzarella cheese

xxxxxxxxxxxxxxxxxxxxxxxxxxxxxxxxxxxxxxxxx

Instructions:

1. Spread tomato sauce on each English muffin half, add tuna, salt and pepper to the taste and sprinkle oregano at the end.

2. Top with mozzarella slices, arrange on a tray, introduce in the oven at 325 degrees F and bake for 3 minutes.

3. Take out of the oven and serve them right away.

Enjoy!

Chapter III - Unique Tuna Soup Recipes

A tuna soup sounds strange? Well, we can assure you that there are some pretty amazing tuna soup recipes out there. Here are the most delicious ones!

XXXXXXXXXXXXXXXXXXXXXXXXXXXXXXXXXXXXXXXX

Recipe 15: Tuna, Beans and Kale Soup

It's very delicious and beautifully colored!

Prep Time: 10 minutes

Total Prep Time: 30 minutes

Serving Sizes:4

List of Ingredients:

- 3 garlic cloves finely chopped
- 1 Tbsp. vegetable oil
- 1 yellow onion finely chopped
- A pinch of red pepper flakes
- 12 ounces canned white tuna, drained and flaked
- 4 cups chicken stock
- 15 ounces canned cannellini beans, drained
- 1 tsp. Italian seasoning
- ½ tsp. paprika
- ½ tsp. fennel seeds
- 1 bunch kale chopped
- Salt and black pepper to the taste
- ¼ cup parmesan cheese, grated

xxxxxxxxxxxxxxxxxxxxxxxxxxxxxxxxxxxxxx

Instructions:

1. Heat up a pan with the oil over medium heat, add onion and cook for 7 minutes stirring from time to time.

2. Add pepper flakes and garlic, stir and cook for 1 minute.

3. Add beans, tuna, stock, Italian seasoning, paprika and fennel, stir, bring to a boil, reduce heat and simmer for 10 minutes.

4. Add kale, stir and simmer for 3 minutes.

5. Add salt and pepper to the taste and the parmesan, stir and cook until it melts.

6. Take off heat, transfer to bowls and serve.

Enjoy!

Recipe 16: Tuna and Potato Soup

It's so easy to make a tasty soup! This next one is the perfect example!

Prep Time: 10 minutes

Total Prep Time: 35 minutes

Serving Sizes: 6

List of Ingredients:

- 2 cups chicken stock
- 2 and ½ cups potatoes diced
- ¼ tsp. sage
- ½ cup yellow onion finely chopped
- ¼ tsp. paprika
- ½ cup carrot diced
- Salt and white pepper to the taste
- ½ cup canned green beans, drained
- 3 cups skim milk
- 6 ounces canned tuna in water, drained and flaked
- ½ cup celery thinly chopped

xxxxxxxxxxxxxxxxxxxxxxxxxxxxxxxxxxxxxxxx

Instructions:

1. In a pot, mix 1 cup potatoes with onions and stock, bring to a boil over medium high heat, cover, reduce temperature to low and simmer for 10 minutes.

2. Add paprika, salt and pepper and sage, stir, take off heat and mash everything.

3. Add the rest of the potatoes, green beans, milk, celery and carrots, stir, bring to a boil over medium high heat, cover, reduce temperature again and simmer for 15 minutes.

4. Add tuna, stir and cook for 5 more minutes.

5. Take soup off heat, transfer to soup bowls and serve.

Enjoy!

Recipe 17: Veggies and Tuna Soup

It's a perfect combination for a perfect day!

Prep Time: 10 minutes

Total Prep Time: 40 minutes

Serving Sizes:6

List of Ingredients:

- 1 Tbsp. vegetable oil
- 1 Tbsp. butter
- 1 small red onion finely chopped
- 2 carrots finely diced
- 2 garlic cloves minced
- 2 zucchinis finely diced
- 2 cups water
- 15 ounces canned tomato sauce
- 2 Tbsp. dried onion
- 2 chicken stock cubes
- 1 tsp. basil
- ½ tsp. oregano
- 1 tsp. parsley
- 1 tsp. dried and ground chili
- 4 ounces canned mushrooms
- 15 ounces canned corn kernels
- 15 ounces canned chickpeas, drained
- 4 ounces canned tuna, drained
- Salt and black pepper to the taste
- 1 cup cheddar cheese, finely grated
- Some fresh cilantro finely chopped for serving

xxxxxxxxxxxxxxxxxxxxxxxxxxxxxxxxxxxxx

Instructions:

1. Heat up a pot with the oil and the butter over high heat, add garlic and onion, stir and cook for 5 minutes.

2. Add zucchini and carrots, stir and cook for 2 minutes.

3. Add dried onion, water, tomato sauce, stock cubes, parsley, oregano, chili and basil, stir, bring to a boil, cover, reduce heat and simmer everything for 20 minutes.

4. Add corn, mushrooms, chickpeas and tuna and simmer for 10 minutes stirring from time to time.

5. Add salt and pepper to the taste, stir, take off heat and pour into soup bowls.

6. Sprinkle grated cheese and cilantro on top and serve.

Enjoy!

Recipe 18: Tuna and Corn Soup

You will ask for more!

Prep Time: 15 minutes

Total Prep Time: 30 minutes

Serving Sizes: 4

List of Ingredients:

- 3 Tbsp. butter
- ½ cup yellow onion diced
- ½ cup celery diced
- 3 Tbsp. white flour
- ¾ cup carrot diced
- 1 tsp. thyme
- 17 ounces canned corn
- 2 cups milk
- 7 ounces canned tuna, drained
- 1 cup bottled clam juice
- Salt and black pepper to the taste

xxxxxxxxxxxxxxxxxxxxxxxxxxxxxxxxxxxxxxxx

Instructions:

1. Put butter in a pot, melt over medium high heat, add onion, carrots and celery, stir and sauté for 5 minutes.

2. Reduce heat, add thyme and white flour, stir and cook for 2 more minutes.

3. Add milk, tuna, corn and clam juice, stir, increase heat to medium high and bring to a simmer.

4. Reduce heat again, add salt and pepper and cook until veggies are done.

5. Transfer to soup bowls and serve.

Enjoy!

Recipe 19: Tasty Tuna Soup

It's a Mediterranean style soup you must make for you and your loved ones!

Prep Time: 5 minutes

Total Prep Time: 20 minutes

Serving Sizes:8

List of Ingredients:

- 2 Tbsp. extra virgin olive oil
- 1 medium squash, diced
- 1 yellow onion finely chopped
- 1 small zucchini chopped
- 28 ounces canned stewed tomatoes, undrained
- 4 garlic cloves finely chopped
- 30 ounces chicken stock
- ½ tsp. oregano
- 8 ounces canned cannelloni beans, undrained
- ¼ cup basil leaves finely chopped
- Salt and black pepper to the taste
- 10 ounces canned white tuna in water, drained
- ½ cup small pasta shells already cooked
- Parmesan cheese, shredded for serving

xxxxxxxxxxxxxxxxxxxxxxxxxxxxxxxxxxxxxx

Instructions:

1. Heat up a pot with the olive oil over medium heat, add garlic and onions, stir and cook for 1-2 minutes.

2. Add squash and zucchini, stir and cook for 2 more minutes.

3. Add tomatoes, chicken stock, salt and pepper, oregano and basil, stir, bring to a boil, cover and simmer for 10 minutes.

4. Add pasta, tuna and beans, stir and cook for 4 more minutes.

5. Pour into bowls, sprinkle cheese on top and serve.

Enjoy!

Recipe 20: Japanese Noodle and Tuna Soup

It's a flavored soup you need to enjoy really soon!

Prep Time: 10 minutes

Total Prep Time: 30 minutes

Serving Sizes: 4

List of Ingredients:

- 1 pint fish stock
- 4 Tbsp. sake
- 4 Tbsp. soy sauce
- 1 Tbsp. caster sugar
- 2 Tbsp. rice wine vinegar
- 2 Tbsp. sesame oil
- 8 ounces straight noodles
- 2 Tbsp. sesame seeds
- 4 tuna steaks
- Coriander leaves chopped for serving

xxxxxxxxxxxxxxxxxxxxxxxxxxxxxxxxxxxxxxxxxxx

Instructions:

1. Put stock in a pot and heat up over medium high heat.

2. Add sake, soy sauce, vinegar, sugar and 1 Tbsp. oil, bring to a boil and simmer for 15 minutes.

3. Brush tuna with the rest of the oil and coat them in sesame seeds.

4. Heat up a pan over high heat, add tuna, cook for 2 minutes on each side and take off heat.

5. Cook noodles according to instructions, drain them and arrange them in soup bowls.

6. Add soup, top with tuna and sprinkle coriander at the end and serve right away.

Recipe 21: Special Broccoli and Tuna Cream Soup

It's full on proteins and other healthy elements!

Prep Time: 5 minutes

Total Prep Time: 20 minutes

Serving Sizes: 5

List of Ingredients:

- 6 ounces canned tuna
- 1 package frozen broccoli florets
- 1 cup yellow onion finely chopped
- ¼ cup butter
- ¼ cup white flour
- 1 cup sour cream
- 2 Tbsp. chives, finely chopped
- 3 cups skim milk
- Salt and black pepper to the taste

XXXXXXXXXXXXXXXXXXXXXXXXXXXXXXXXXXXXXXXXX

Instructions:

1. Heat up a pot with the butter over medium heat, add onions and cook for 6-7 minutes stirring from time to time.

2. Add flour and skim milk, stir and bring to a boil.

3. Add tuna, broccoli, salt and pepper to the taste, stir and simmer for 13 minutes.

4. Add sour cream and chives, stir, bring to a simmer, take off heat, pour into soup bowls and serve hot.

Enjoy!

Chapter IV - Incredible Tuna Appetizer Recipes

Those tuna breakfast ideas were pretty great, right? Then, it's time we help you learn more amazing tuna recipes. Pay attention and discover some incredible tuna appetizers.

Recipe 22: Amazing Tuna Spread

Spread this on crackers, arrange them on a platter and serve them for your next party!

Prep Time: 10 minutes

Total Prep Time: 10 minutes

Serving Sizes: 12

List of Ingredients:

- 6 ounces canned tuna, drained and flaked
- 3 tsp. lemon juice
- 1 tsp. onion salt
- 8 ounces soft cream cheese
- 4 drops hot pepper sauce
- ¼ cup parsley finely chopped

XXXXXXXXXXXXXXXXXXXXXXXXXXXXXXXXXXXXXX

Instructions:

1. In a bowl, mix tuna with cream cheese, lemon juice, hot pepper sauce and onion salt and stir well.

2. Shape a big ball, roll in chopped parsley, and keep in the fridge until you serve.

3. Transfer to a platter, arrange crackers all around and serve.

Enjoy!

Recipe 23: Elegant Tuna Appetizer

It's a really special appetizer! Try it soon!

Prep Time: 10 minutes

Total Prep Time: 10 minutes

Serving Sizes:3

List of Ingredients:

- 7 ounces sashimi grade tuna cubed
- 4 cherry tomatoes cubed
- 1/3 cucumber cubed
- 1 dash coriander leaves
- 4 Tbsp. extra virgin olive oil
- Salt and black pepper to the taste
- 3 Tbsp. vinegar
- 1 tsp. lemon juice

XXXXXXXXXXXXXXXXXXXXXXXXXXXXXXXXXXXXXXXX

Instructions:

1. In a bowl, mix tuna with salt, black pepper and 2 Tbsp. olive oil and toss to coat.

2. Keep in the fridge for a while.

3. In another bowl, mix cucumber with tomatoes, 2 Tbsp. oil, salt, pepper and 3 Tbsp. vinegar.

4. Also keep this in the fridge for a while.

5. Put a round mold on a plate, add tuna on the bottom and press, add vegetables on top and press again.

6. Add coriander leaves and the marinade from the veggies, take mold off, add lemon juice and serve.

Enjoy!

Recipe 24: Delicious Tuna Kabobs

They look amazing and they taste divine!

Prep Time: 30 minutes

Total Prep Time: 40 minutes

Serving Sizes:16

List of Ingredients:

- ¼ cup soy sauce
- 1 pound tuna steaks, cubed in 16 pieces
- 2 Tbsp. rice vinegar
- Salt and black pepper to the taste
- 1 Tbsp. sesame seeds
- 2 Tbsp. canola oil
- 16 pieces pickled ginger
- ½ cup wasabi mayo
- 1 bunch watercress

XXXXXXXXXXXXXXXXXXXXXXXXXXXXXXXXXXXXXXXXX

Instructions:

1. In a bowl, mix soy sauce with vinegar and tuna, toss to coat, cover bowl and keep in the fridge for 30 minutes.

2. Discard marinade, pat dry tuna and sprinkle it with salt, black pepper and sesame seeds.

3. Heat up a pan with the oil over medium heat, add tuna pieces, cook them until they are pink in the center and browned on the outside, take them off heat and transfer them to a plate.

4. Thread one ginger slice on each of the 16 skewers.

5. Thread one tuna cube on each of the 16 skewers.

6. Arrange watercress on a platter, arrange tuna kabobs on top and serve with wasabi mayo on the side.

Enjoy!

Recipe 25: Tuna Carpaccio

It's an elegant appetizer you just need to try!

Prep Time: 10 minutes

Total Prep Time: 10 minutes

Serving Sizes: 2

List of Ingredients:

- 7 ounces tuna, very thinly sliced
- 1 tomato chopped
- 1 tsp. parsley finely chopped
- 1 avocado, pitted and chopped
- 1 tsp. extra virgin olive oil
- Salt and black pepper to the taste
- 1 tsp. lemon juice

xxxxxxxxxxxxxxxxxxxxxxxxxxxxxxxxxxxxxxxxxx

Instructions:

1. Put tomato in a bowl, add salt and pepper to the taste and half of the lemon juice and stir.

2. Put avocado in another bowl, add salt and pepper to the taste and the rest of the lemon juice and stir.

3. Combine tomato and avocado, stir and mix with the olive oil and the parsley.

4. Arrange tuna on a serving platter, sprinkle salt and pepper and arrange the avocado and tomato mix in the middle.

5. Serve right away.

Enjoy!

Recipe 26: Special Tuna Bites

It's a fresh Asian style tuna appetizer you will definitely enjoy!

Prep Time: 10 minutes

Total Prep Time: 15 minutes

Serving Sizes:30

List of Ingredients:

- 2 Tbsp. red wine vinegar
- 3 Tbsp. mustard
- 1 Tbsp. sesame soil
- 2 Tbsp. soy sauce
- 1 tsp. hot pepper sauce
- 1 pound tuna steaks, cut in 30 cubes
- ¼ cup sesame oil
- Cooking spray
- Salt and black pepper to the taste
- 2 green onions finely chopped

xxxxxxxxxxxxxxxxxxxxxxxxxxxxxxxxxxxxxxxx

Instructions:

1. In a bowl, mix mustard with vinegar, soy sauce, sesame oil and hot pepper sauce and stir well.

2. Spray some cooking oil on each tuna cube, sprinkle them with sesame seeds and put them on a plate.

3. Heat up a pan with some cooking spray over medium high heat, add tuna pieces, brown them on the outside and make sure they're pink on the inside and take them off heat.

4. Thread 1 tuna cube on a skewer and repeat this with the rest of the cubes.

5. Arrange them on a platter, sprinkle onions all over and serve them.

Enjoy!

Recipe 27: Delightful Tuna Pate

It's such an easy appetizer! You'll see!

Prep Time: 5 minutes

Total Prep Time: 5 minutes

Serving Sizes: 12

List of Ingredients:

- 6 ounces canned tuna, drained and flaked
- ½ cup almonds, thinly sliced and toasted
- 1 yellow onion, cut in quarters
- 2 hardboiled eggs
- 4 gherkins
- Salt and black pepper to the taste
- 1 dash Tabasco sauce
- 1/3 cup homemade mayonnaise
- 1 tsp. Worcestershire sauce

For serving:

- 1 egg, hard boiled and thinly sliced
- Crackers
- Some chopped parsley

xxxxxxxxxxxxxxxxxxxxxxxxxxxxxxxxxxxxxxxx

Instructions:

1. In your food processor, mix tuna with onion, almonds, 2 eggs, gherkins, salt and black pepper to the taste, mayo, Worcestershire and Tabasco sauce and blend very well.

2. Transfer to a bowl, cover and keep in the fridge for 6 hours.

3. Transfer to serving bowls, garnish with egg slices and parsley and serve with crackers.

Enjoy!

Recipe 28: Tuna and Cucumber Appetizer

It's a very healthy tuna appetizer you can make for your next party!

Prep Time: 10 minutes

Total Prep Time: 10 minutes

Serving Sizes:20

List of Ingredients:

- 2/3 cup canned tuna, drained and flaked
- 2 and ½ Tbsp. red onions finely chopped
- 2 Tbsp. homemade mayo
- 1 tsp. parsley finely chopped
- Salt and black pepper to the taste
- 2 cucumbers cut into 1 inch thick rounds
- Chili powder for serving

xxxxxxxxxxxxxxxxxxxxxxxxxxxxxxxxxxxxxxx

Instructions:

1. Scoop pulp from cucumber rounds but leave some on the bottom to form a cup, arrange them on a platter and leave them aside.

2. In a bowl, mix tuna with red onions, mayo, parsley, salt and pepper to the taste and stir well.

3. Spoon this tuna mix in cucumber cups, sprinkle chili powder on top and serve right away.

Enjoy!

Chapter V - Amazing and Beautiful Tuna Steak Dishes

These next tuna dishes are simply perfect. Get ready to discover some really impressive recipes and make sure you try them all.

XXXXXXXXXXXXXXXXXXXXXXXXXXXXXXXXXXXXXXXXXX

Recipe 29: Amazing Crusted Tuna Steaks

This dish doesn't just look wonderful! It also tastes amazing!

Prep Time: 10 minutes

Total Prep Time: 20 minutes

Serving Sizes:2

List of Ingredients:

- 2 Tbsp. extra virgin olive oil
- 2 ahi tuna steaks
- 3 Tbsp. black sesame seeds
- 3 Tbsp. white sesame seeds
- 1 tsp. sesame oil
- Salt and black pepper to the taste

For the mango and avocado salsa:

- ½ white onion finely chopped
- 2 cups tomatoes diced
- ¼ cup cilantro finely chopped
- 1 jalapeno pepper finely chopped
- 2 garlic cloves finely chopped
- Juice from 1 lime
- 1 Tbsp. lime juice
- 1 avocado, cut in halves
- 1 tsp. white wine vinegar
- 1 mango, cut in halves
- 2 Tbsp. canola oil
- Cumin to the taste
- Cayenne pepper to the taste
- Salt and black pepper to the taste

XXXXXXXXXXXXXXXXXXXXXXXXXXXXXXXXXXXXXXX

Instructions:

1. In a bowl, mix olive oil with sesame oil and stir.

2. Brush tuna steaks and put them on a plate.

3. In a bowl, mix black and with sesame seeds and salt and pepper to the taste and stir.

4. Cover tuna steaks with sesame seeds mix.

5. Heat up your kitchen grill over high heat and place steaks on it.

6. Cook for 2 minutes on each side, transfer to a cutting board, leave aside to cool down and slice.

7. Meanwhile, in a bowl, mix onion with tomato, cilantro, garlic, lime juice, jalapeno and vinegar.

8. Brush avocado and mango halves with canola oil, drizzle 1 Tbsp. lime juice over them, place on heated grill and cook for 3-4 minutes, turning them after 2 minutes.

9. Peel grilled avocado and mango, finely chop them and add them to the rest of the veggies.

10. Add salt, pepper, cayenne pepper and cumin, stir well and keep in the fridge until you serve it.

11. Arrange tuna slices on a platter and serve with your chilled mango and avocado salsa.

Enjoy!

Recipe 30: Tuna Steak and Tasty Brandy Sauce

It's a Japanese style dish that will soon become one of your favorite ones!

Prep Time: 6 minutes

Total Prep Time: 12 minutes

Serving Sizes:2

List of Ingredients:

- 6 ounces sushi tuna steak
- Salt and black pepper to the taste
- 1 Tbsp. sugar
- 1 ounce brandy
- 2 and ½ Tbsp. soy sauce
- 1 Tbsp. mirin
- ¼ cup heavy cream
- Green onion finely chopped for serving
- Some fried spaghetti for serving

XXXXXXXXXXXXXXXXXXXXXXXXXXXXXXXXXXXXXXX

Instructions:

1. Put soy sauce, sugar, brandy and mirin in a pan, heat up over medium high heat, bring to a boil and cook until it's reduces.

2. Add cream, stir, cook until it thickens, take off heat and leave aside to cool down.

3. Heat up a pan over medium high heat, grease it with some cooking spray, season tuna with salt and pepper to the taste and add it to the pan.

4. Cook for 3 minutes, flip and cook for 3 more minutes, transfer to a cutting board and cut in very thin slices.

5. Arrange slices in bowls, add fried spaghetti over them, add some of the sauce and top with green onions.

Recipe 31: Grilled Marinated Tuna Steak

It's so juicy and delicious!

Prep Time: 30 minutes

Total Prep Time: 40 minutes

Serving Sizes: 4

List of Ingredients:

- ¼ cup orange juice
- 1 garlic clove finely chopped
- ¼ cup soy sauce
- 1 Tbsp. lemon juice
- 2 Tbsp. extra virgin olive oil
- Salt and black pepper to the taste
- 2 Tbsp. parslcy finely chopped
- ½ tsp. oregano finely chopped
- 4 medium tuna steaks
- Grilled artichoke hearts for serving

xxxxxxxxxxxxxxxxxxxxxxxxxxxxxxxxxxxxxxxx

Instructions:

1. In a dish mix orange juice with olive oil, soy sauce, lemon juice, oregano, salt and pepper to the taste, parsley and garlic and stir.

2. Add tuna steaks, toss to coat, cover and keep in the fridge for 30 minutes.

3. Heat up your kitchen grill over medium high heat, add steaks, cook for 6 minutes, flip, baste with some of the marinade, cook for 5 more minutes and transfer to plates.

4. Serve with grilled artichoke hearts right away.

Enjoy!

Recipe 32: The Best Tuna with Wasabi Cream

You'll be so happy when you'll try this tuna dish!

Prep Time: 1 hour

Total Prep Time: 1 hour and 10 minutes

Serving Sizes: 2

List of Ingredients:

- 2 Tbsp. soy sauce
- ½ tsp. ginger finely grated
- 1 garlic clove finely chopped
- 2 Tbsp. sweet cooking rice wine
- 1 tsp. sesame oil
- 2 Tbsp. extra virgin olive oil
- 2 ahi tuna steaks
- ¼ cup sour cream
- 1 tsp. rice vinegar
- 1 tsp. wasabi paste

XXXXXXXXXXXXXXXXXXXXXXXXXXXXXXXXXXXXXXX

Instructions:

1. In a bowl, mix sesame oil with soy sauce, rice wine, garlic and ginger and stir well.

2. Add tuna steaks to this mix, toss to coat, cover and keep in the fridge for 1 hour.

3. In another bowl, mix sour cream with vinegar and wasabi paste, stir well, cover and keep in the fridge until you serve it.

4. Heat up a pan with the olive oil over medium high heat, add tuna steaks, cook for 3 minutes on each side, transfer to a cutting board, leave aside for a few minutes, slice and arrange on a platter.

5. Spoon wasabi cream all over and serve.

Recipe 33: Amazing Seared Tuna Steak

Everyone will admire you once you make this dish!

Prep Time: 5 minutes

Total Prep Time: 15 minutes

Serving Sizes: 2

List of Ingredients:

- 2 ahi tuna steaks
- ¼ tsp. cayenne pepper
- ½ Tbsp. butter
- Salt to the taste
- 2 Tbsp. extra virgin olive oil
- 1 tsp. whole peppercorns

xxxxxxxxxxxxxxxxxxxxxxxxxxxxxxxxxxxxxxxx

Instructions:

1. Season tuna steaks with cayenne pepper and salt to the taste, place them on a plate and leave aside for now.

2. Heat up a pan with the oil over medium high heat, add butter and melt it.

3. Add peppercorns, stir and cook for 5 minutes.

4. Add tuna steaks and cook for 1 and ½ minutes on each side.

5. Transfer to a platter, cut and serve with your favorite side salad.

Enjoy!

Recipe 34: Tuna with Potatoes and Tomatoes

Two words can characterize this dish: fresh and savory!

Prep Time: 10 minutes

Total Prep Time: 40 minutes

Serving Sizes:4

List of Ingredients:

- 1 Tbsp. extra-virgin olive oil
- 3 garlic cloves finely chopped
- 4 medium tuna steaks
- Some thyme springs torn
- 17 ounces baby potatoes, sliced
- 1 red onion cut in 8 pieces
- 2 red bell peppers cut in chunks
- 1 green chili pepper chopped
- 16 ounces canned cherry tomatoes
- Salt and black pepper to the taste

Instructions:

1. Put tuna steaks in a dish, add half of the oil, 2 garlic cloves, 2 thyme springs, toss to coat and leave aside for now.

2. Put potatoes in a baking pan and mix with red bell pepper, onion, chili pepper, the rest of the oil, salt and pepper to the taste, toss to coat, introduce in the oven at 370 degrees F and bake for 20 minutes.

3. Take pan out of the oven, add the rest of the thyme, the rest of the garlic, stir and heat up on the stove over medium high heat.

4. Add tomatoes, more salt and pepper if needed, stir and cook for 5 minutes.

5. Heat up your kitchen grill over medium high heat, discard marinade from tuna steaks, pat dry them, season with salt and pepper to the taste, place on grill and cook for 2 minutes on each side.

6. Transfer steaks to plates and serve with roasted veggies on the side.

Enjoy!

Recipe 35: Amazing Grilled Tuna with Horseradish Sauce

The flavors transform this dish into a real feast!

Prep Time: 20 minutes

Total Prep Time: 27 minutes

Serving Sizes: 2

List of Ingredients:

- 1 tsp. vegetable oil
- 2 tuna steaks
- 2 Tbsp. soy sauce
- 2 Tbsp. rice vinegar
- ½ tsp. hot chili paste
- 4 cherry tomatoes thinly sliced
- 1 Tbsp. raw horseradish root finely grated
- 1 Tbsp. green onions finely chopped
- Salt and black pepper to the taste

XXXXXXXXXXXXXXXXXXXXXXXXXXXXXXXXXXXXXXXX

Instructions:

1. Heat up your kitchen grill over medium high heat and grease it a little bit.

2. Season tuna with salt and pepper and grease them with vegetable oil.

3. Meanwhile, in a bowl, mix soy sauce with horseradish, vinegar, hot chili paste and tomatoes, stir and leave aside for 20 minutes.

4. Place tuna steaks on grill, cook for 3 minutes, flip and cook for 3 more minutes and transfer to a plate.

5. Spread the horseradish and tomatoes sauce on top, sprinkle green onion and serve.

Enjoy!

Recipe 36: Grilled Tuna Steaks with Beans

The herbs used for this dish make it perfect!

Prep Time: 10 minutes

Total Prep Time: 30 minutes

Serving Sizes: 4

List of Ingredients:

- 4 medium tuna steaks
- A drizzle of extra virgin olive oil
- Salt and black pepper to the taste
- Lemon wedges for serving

For the beans:

- 2 garlic cloves finely chopped
- 2 Tbsp. extra virgin olive oil
- 2 canes cannellini beans, drained
- 1 red pepper, roasted and chopped
- 1 yellow onion finely chopped
- 2 rosemary springs chopped
- A handful parsley finely chopped
- Salt and black pepper to the taste

For the bitter beans:

- 1 head of radicchio, shredded
- 1 head escarole, shredded
- A drizzle of olive oil
- Salt to the taste
- Juice from 1 lemon

XXXXXXXXXXXXXXXXXXXXXXXXXXXXXXXXXXXXXXX

Instructions:

1. Heat up a pan over medium high heat, pat dry tuna steaks, season with salt and black pepper, add them to pan, drizzle some olive oil over them, cook for 2 minutes, flip, cover pan with tin foil and cook for 6 more minutes.

2. Take off heat and keep steaks covered.

3. Heat up another pan over medium heat, add 2 Tbsp. olive oil, 2 garlic cloves and 1 chopped onion, stir and cook for 3 minutes.

4. Add cannellini beans and roasted pepper, stir and cook for 3 minutes.

5. Add rosemary spring, a handful parsley, salt, pepper, stir and cook for 2 more minutes.

6. Meanwhile, in a bowl, mix escarole with radicchio, a drizzle of olive oil, salt to the taste and lemon juice and toss to coat.

7. Transfer tuna steaks to plates, add cannellini beans on top and serve with bitter beans salad on the side. Enjoy!

Recipe 37: Tasty Tuna Steaks with Cucumber Relish

It's full of healthy ingredients!

Prep Time: 30 minutes

Total Prep Time: 35 minutes

Serving Sizes: 4

List of Ingredients:

- 4 medium tuna steaks
- 3 Tbsp. extra virgin olive oil

For the cucumber relish:

- 2 spring onions, finely chopped
- 1 small cucumber chopped
- 1 tomato fincly chopped
- ½ red chili pepper, finely chopped
- 2 Tbsp. parsley finely chopped
- 1 Tbsp. extra virgin olive oil
- 1 Tbsp. lemon juice
- Salt and black pepper to the taste

XXXXXXXXXXXXXXXXXXXXXXXXXXXXXXXXXXXXX

Instructions:

1. Put tuna steaks in a bag, add 3 Tbsp. olive oil, seal bag, shake and leave aside for 30 minutes.

2. In a bowl, mix cucumber with salt, pepper to the taste, spring onions, tomato, chili pepper, 1 Tbsp. oil, parsley and lemon juice and stir well.

3. Heat up your kitchen grill over medium high heat, add steaks, cook for 2 minutes, flip them and cook for another 2 minutes.

4. Transfer steaks to plates, leave aside for 4 minutes, spoon cucumber relish on top and serve.

Recipe 38: Tuna Steaks with Olives, Peppers, Tomato and Capers

Get ready to experience an Italian style tuna dish!

Prep Time: 10 minutes

Total Prep Time: 35 minutes

Serving Sizes:4

List of Ingredients:

- 3 garlic cloves thinly chopped
- 3 Tbsp. extra virgin olive oil
- 1 and ½ pounds albacore tune, cut in thin strips
- ½ cup red onion thinly sliced
- 1 Tbsp. mint leaves finely chopped
- 1 Tbsp. basil finely chopped
- 1 tsp. fresh oregano finely chopped
- Salt and black pepper to the taste
- ½ cup kalamata olives pitted and chopped
- 1 cup tomatoes, chopped
- A pinch red pepper flakes
- 1 Tbsp. capers, drained
- Some fresh basil chopped for serving
- Some mint leaves chopped for serving

XXXXXXXXXXXXXXXXXXXXXXXXXXXXXXXXXXXXXX

Instructions:

1. Heat up a pan with the olive oil over medium high heat, add garlic, stir and cook for 15 minutes, transfer to a bowl and leave aside.

2. Add red onions to the same pan, stir and cook for 2 minutes.

3. Add tuna strips, increase heat to high and cook for 1-2 minutes.

4. Add basil, oregano and mint, salt and pepper to the taste, stir and cook for 3 minutes, transfer to a platter and keep warm.

5. Return garlic to pan, add capers, pepper flakes, olives and tomatoes, stir and cook for 1 minute.

6. Pour this over tuna strips, sprinkle some basil and mint on top and serve.

Enjoy!

Recipe 39: Tuscan Style Tuna Steaks

This dish is a good choice for a weekend dinner!

Prep Time: 10 minutes

Total Prep Time: 25 minutes

Serving Sizes:4

List of Ingredients:

- 3 springs fresh rosemary
- Zest from 1 lemon
- 3 garlic cloves crushed
- Salt and black pepper to the taste
- A drizzle of extra virgin olive oil
- 4 medium tuna steaks
- A handful parsley leaves

XXXXXXXXXXXXXXXXXXXXXXXXXXXXXXXXXXXXXXX

Instructions:

1. Rinse and pat dry tuna steaks and put them on a plate.

2. Put lemon zest on a cutting board, add rosemary and parsley on top.

3. Also add salt and pepper and chopped garlic and chop everything.

4. Drizzle olive oil over tuna steaks, rub them with herbs mix and leave aside for 10 minutes.

5. Heat up your kitchen grill over medium high heat, add tuna steaks and cook them for 6 minutes on each side.

6. Transfer to plates, cut and serve right away.

Enjoy!

Recipe 40: Tasty Tuna Steaks with Tomatoes and Basil Sauce

It's so easy to make a healthy and tasty dinner! Try this idea tonight!

Prep Time: 10 minutes

Total Prep Time: 20 minutes

Serving Sizes: 4

List of Ingredients:

- 4 medium tuna steaks
- 3 Tbsp. extra virgin olive oil
- Salt and black pepper to the taste
- 1 red onion finely chopped
- 6 plum tomatoes finely chopped
- A handful parsley finely chopped
- ½ cup basil finely chopped

xxxxxxxxxxxxxxxxxxxxxxxxxxxxxxxxxxxxxxxx

Instructions:

1. Heat up your kitchen grill over medium high heat, season tuna steaks with salt and pepper to the taste, brush them with 1 Tbsp. olive oil, place them on grill, cook for 3 minutes on each side, transfer to a platter and leave aside for now.

2. In a bowl, mix parsley with basil, onions and tomatoes.

3. Add salt and pepper to the taste, 2 Tbsp. olive oil, toss to coat and leave aside for 10 minutes.

4. Arrange tuna steaks on plates, top each with some of the basil and tomatoes mix and serve. Enjoy!

Recipe 41: Amazing Tuna Steak with a Special Marinade

It's a really special tuna dish!

Prep Time: 2 hours

Total Prep Time: 2 hours and 8 minutes

Serving Sizes: 1

List of Ingredients:

- 1 big tuna steak
- 3 Tbsp. coconut oil
- ½ cup cilantro finely chopped
- 1 tsp. ginger finely grated
- 2 garlic cloves finely chopped
- Zest from 1 lime
- Juice from 1 lime
- 4 cups baby spinach leaves
- Salt and black pepper to the taste
- ½ avocado, pitted and sliced

xxxxxxxxxxxxxxxxxxxxxxxxxxxxxxxxxxxxxxx

Instructions:

1. In a bowl, mix oil with garlic, ginger, lime juice, lime zest and cilantro and stir well.

2. Season tuna steaks with salt and black pepper to the taste, put them in the marinade you've made, cover and leave in the fridge for 2 hours.

3. Heat up your grill over medium high heat, add tuna steak, and cook for 4 minutes on each side.

4. Meanwhile, heat up another pan over medium heat after you've greased it a little bit, add spinach and cook for 2-3 minutes.

5. Add salt and pepper to the taste and transfer to a bowl.

6. Heat up the same pan over medium heat, add the marinade from the tuna steak and cook until it thickens.

7. Arrange sautéed spinach on a plate, add tuna, add sliced avocado and the sauce you've just made.

Enjoy!

Recipe 42: Pan Fried and Glazed Tuna Steaks

It's one of the best ways to cook tuna steaks!

Prep Time: 10 minutes

Total Prep Time: 20 minutes

Serving Sizes:4

List of Ingredients:

- 4 medium tuna steaks
- 1 Tbsp. soy sauce
- 1 Tbsp. honey
- 1 Tbsp. extra-virgin olive oil

For the veggies:

- 1 red onion chopped
- 1 red bell pepper chopped
- 1 green bell pepper chopped
- 8 mushrooms thinly sliced
- 4 spring onions chopped
- 1 Tbsp. sesame oil
- 2 garlic cloves finely chopped
- 1 Tbsp. soy sauce
- 1 inch piece ginger finely cut in strips

XXXXXXXXXXXXXXXXXXXXXXXXXXXXXXXXXXXXXX

Instructions:

1. In a bowl, mix tuna steaks with honey, 1 Tbsp. soy sauce and some of the oil and toss to coat.

2. Brush a pan with the rest of the oil, heat up over medium high heat, add tuna steaks, cook for 3 minutes on each side, take off heat and transfer to plates.

3. Heat up a pan with the sesame oil over medium high heat, add ginger, stir and cook for 1 minute.

4. Add red and green bell peppers, red onion, spring onions, mushrooms and garlic, stir and cook for 5-6 minutes.

5. Add 1 Tbsp. soy sauce, stir and cook for 1 more minute.

6. Serve tuna steaks with the veggies you've prepared on the side.

Enjoy!

Recipe 43: Tuna Steaks with Mustard and Vinegar Vinaigrette

This vinaigrette gives tuna such an amazing taste and flavor!

Prep Time: 10 minutes

Total Prep Time: 18 minutes

Serving Sizes:6

List of Ingredients:

- 6 tuna steaks
- 3 Tbsp. red wine vinegar+1 tsp. more
- Salt and black to the taste
- 2 tsp. honey
- 2 Tbsp. Dijon mustard
- ¾ cup extra virgin olive oil
- 2 Tbsp. thyme finely chopped
- Vegetable oil for the grill

xxxxxxxxxxxxxxxxxxxxxxxxxxxxxxxxxxxxxxx

Instructions:

1. In a bowl, mix vinegar with salt, honey, thyme and mustard in a bowl.

2. Add olive oil gradually and stir until everything combines.

3. Brush tuna steaks with ¾ cup vinaigrette, season them with salt and pepper to the taste, place on heated grill, cook for 4 minutes on each side and transfer to a platter.

4. Drizzle the rest of the vinaigrette on top and serve.

Enjoy!

Chapter VI - The Most Delicious Tuna Casserole Recipes

There's nothing more comforting than a good tuna casserole. Here are the best tuna casserole recipes especially gathered for you!

xxxxxxxxxxxxxxxxxxxxxxxxxxxxxxxxxxxxxxxxxx

Recipe 44: Tuna and Egg Casserole

It's a fantastic tuna casserole even you kids will love!

Prep Time: 5 minutes

Total Prep Time: 40 minutes

Serving Sizes:4

List of Ingredients:

- 1 and ½ cups light margarine
- 1 and ½ cups basmati rice
- 1 yellow onion finely chopped
- 1 cup milk
- 2 Tbsp. white flour
- 1 tsp. dry mustard
- 1 cup chicken stock
- 2 celery stalks finely chopped
- 4 hardboiled eggs, chopped
- 2 tomatoes sliced
- 2 tomatoes finely chopped
- 7 ounces canned tuna, drained
- Cooking spray

XXXXXXXXXXXXXXXXXXXXXXXXXXXXXXXXXXXXXX

Instructions:

1. Heat up a pan over medium heat, add margarine and melt it.

2. Add onion, celery, salt and pepper to the taste, stir and cook for 5 minutes.

3. Add flour, stir and cook for 1 more minute.

4. Add stock and milk and stir well.

5. Add mustard, bring to a simmer, cook for 2 minutes and take off heat.

6. Add tuna, chopped tomatoes, eggs, more salt and pepper and rice, stir and pour this into a baking dish greased with some cooking spray.

7. Top with sliced tomatoes, introduce in the oven at 350 degrees F and bake for 25 minutes.

8. Take casserole out of the oven, leave aside for a few minutes, cut, arrange on plates and serve.

Enjoy!

Recipe 45: Delicious Tuna and Shrimp Casserole

If you are a seafood fan, than this casserole is perfect for you!

Prep Time: 15 minutes

Total Prep Time: 1 hour and 35 minutes

Serving Sizes:8

List of Ingredients:

- 3 cups wide egg noodles
- Salt and black pepper to the taste
- 1 pound shrimp, deveined and peeled
- 2 Tbsp. soft butter
- 2 and ½ cups milk
- 1 and ½ Tbsp. white flour
- ½ cup heavy cream
- 5 ounces canned mushrooms, drained and sliced
- 1 cup green peas, frozen
- 1 cup buttery round crackers crumbled
- 1 Tbsp. cold butter, sliced
- Cooking spray

XXXXXXXXXXXXXXXXXXXXXXXXXXXXXXXXXXXXXX

Instructions:

1. Put water in a pot, bring to a boil over the high heat, add shrimp, reduce heat, cook for 3 minutes, transfer shrimp to a bowl and leave aside for now.

2. Return pot with water to heat, bring to a boil over high heat again, add noodles, cook for 8 minutes, drain, rinse and put them in a bowl.

3. Heat up a pan with 2 Tbsp. soft butter over medium heat, add flour, stir well to obtain a paste, take off heat and mix well with cream and milk.

4. Add salt and pepper to the taste, return to reduced heat and simmer for 5 minutes stirring all the time.

5. Grease a baking dish with some cooking spray, pour noodles on the bottom and spread.

6. Add mushrooms, peas and shrimp.

7. Add sauce you've just prepared on top and sprinkle cracker crumbs at the end.

8. Add the sliced butter, introduce casserole in the oven at 350 degrees F and bake for 1 hour.

9. Take casserole out of the oven, leave aside to cool down for a few minutes, cut, transfer to plates and serve.

Enjoy!

Recipe 46: The Most Amazing Tuna Casserole

It's a tuna casserole worth trying!

Prep Time: 10 minutes

Total Prep Time: 30 minutes

Serving Sizes:6

List of Ingredients:

- 12 ounces egg noodles
- 2 cups cheddar cheese, shredded
- ¼ cup yellow onion finely chopped
- 1 cup frozen green peas
- 3 ounce canned mushrooms thinly sliced
- 1 cup potato chips crushed
- 21 ounces canned condensed cream of mushroom soup
- 12 ounces canned tuna, drained
- Salt and black pepper to the taste

xxxxxxxxxxxxxxxxxxxxxxxxxxxxxxxxxxxxxxx

Instructions:

1. Put water in a pot, add salt, bring to a boil, add noodles, cook for 8 minutes, drain and transfer them to a bowl.

2. Add onion, 1 cup cheese, tuna, soup, peas and mushrooms and stir well.

3. Transfer to a baking dish, season with salt and pepper to the taste, top with the rest of the cheese and the potato chips, spread them, introduce in the oven at 425 degrees F and bake for 15 minutes.

4. Take out of the oven, cut, put on serving plates and serve right away.

Enjoy!

Recipe 47: Tuna and Spinach Casserole

It's a classic dish with a modern twist! You just have to try it!

Prep Time: 20 minutes

Total Prep Time: 45 minutes

Serving Sizes: 8

List of Ingredients:

- 18 ounces canned creamy mushroom soup
- 2 cups cheddar cheese shredded
- 5 cups egg noodles
- 12 ounces canned tuna in water, drained
- ½ cup milk
- 9 ounces frozen spinach, chopped
- 2 tsp. lemon peel finely grated
- 8 ounces refrigerated dinner rolls dough
- Cooking spray

XXXXXXXXXXXXXXXXXXXXXXXXXXXXXXXXXXXXXXX

Instructions:

1. Put water in a pot, add salt, bring to a boil over medium high heat, add noodles, cook according to package instructions, drain, rinse and put in a bowl.

2. Put mushroom soup in a pan, heat up over medium high heat, add 1 and ½ cups cheddar cheese, stir and cook until it melts.

3. Add tuna, noodles, milk, spinach and lemon peel, stir and cook for 3-4 minutes.

4. Transfer mix to a baking dish which you've greased with cooking spray.

5. Unroll dinner rolls dough, sprinkle the rest of the cheese on them, roll up again, seal edges, cut in 8 pieces and place them on top of tuna casserole mix.

6. Introduce in the oven at 375 degrees F and bake for 25 minutes.

7. Take out of the oven, leave aside to cool down a bit, cut and serve.

Enjoy!

Recipe 48: Rich Tuna Casserole

Are you looking for a rich tuna casserole? Stop looking! This is it!

Prep Time: 10 minutes

Total Prep Time: 55 minutes

Serving Sizes:6

List of Ingredients:

- 12 ounces canned tuna, drained and flaked
- 3 cups egg noodles
- ½ tsp. thyme
- ½ cup homemade mayonnaise
- ½ cup celery finely chopped
- Salt and black pepper to the taste
- 1/3 cup green onions finely chopped
- 1/3 cup sour cream
- 1 zucchini sliced
- 1 cup Monterey Jack cheese, shredded
- 2 tsp. mustard
- 1 tomato finely chopped

XXXXXXXXXXXXXXXXXXXXXXXXXXXXXXXXXXXXXXX

Instructions:

1. Put water in a pot, add salt, bring to a boil over medium heat, add noodles, cook according to instructions, drain and transfer to a bowl.

2. Mix noodles with celery, tuna and green onions and stir.

3. Also add mustard, mayo and sour cream and stir well.

4. Add salt and pepper to the taste and thyme and stir again.

5. Pour half of this mix into a baking dish, arrange a layer of zucchini slices, add the rest of the noodles mix and spread.

6. Add another layer of zucchini, top with cheese, introduce in the oven at 350 degrees F and bake for 30 minutes.

7. Take casserole out of the oven, cut and arrange on plates and serve with tomato slices on top.

Enjoy!

Recipe 49: Tuna and Tomato Casserole

It's a hearty tuna casserole you should try tonight!

Prep Time: 10 minutes

Total Prep Time: 50 minutes

Serving Sizes:4

List of Ingredients:

- 9 ounces shell pasta
- 1 Tbsp. extra-virgin olive oil
- Salt and black pepper to the taste
- ¾ cup pureed tomato
- 1 and ½ cups milk
- 3 Tbsp. white flour
- 4 Tbsp. mozzarella cheese, grated
- 2 ounces canned tuna, drained
- 2 Tbsp. parsley finely chopped

XXXXXXXXXXXXXXXXXXXXXXXXXXXXXXXXXXXXXXX

Instructions:

1. Put water in a pot, add salt, bring to a boil over medium high heat, add pasta, cook for 8 minutes, drain, transfer to a bowl and leave aside.

2. Heat up a pan with the oil over medium high heat, add tomato puree, stir and simmer for 5 minutes.

3. Add milk and flour, stir well, bring to a boil, reduce heat to low and simmer until it thickens.

4. Add tuna and stir again.

5. Add pasta, mix everything, pour into a baking dish, season with salt and pepper, sprinkle mozzarella and parsley on top, introduce in the oven at 370 degrees F and bake for 20 minutes.

6. Take casserole out of the oven, leave aside for a few minutes, cut, transfer to plates and serve.

Recipe 50: Delicious Creamy Tuna and Avocado Casserole

It's a very classy dish you will enjoy!

Prep Time: 10 minutes

Total Prep Time: 45 minutes

Serving Sizes:8

List of Ingredients:

- 2 big avocados pitted and cubed
- 2 cups dry whole grain penne paste
- 2 cups dry regular penne pasta
- 3 Tbsp. lemon juice
- 1 and ½ cups milk
- 1 tsp. oregano
- 3 garlic cloves finely sliced
- 1 red bell pepper finely diced
- ¾ cup parsley roughly chopped
- ¾ cup parmesan cheese shredded
- Salt and black pepper to the taste
- 12 ounces canned white tuna, drained and flaked

For the breadcrumbs:

- 2 slices whole wheat bread, toasted and crumbled
- 1 tsp. extra virgin olive oil
- ¼ tsp. paprika
- ¼ tsp. garlic powder
- Cooking spray

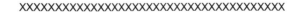

xxxxxxxxxxxxxxxxxxxxxxxxxxxxxxxxxxxxxxxx

Instructions:

1. Put avocado pieces in a bowl, mix with lemon juice and toss to coat.

2. Cook regular pasta and whole grain pasta according to instructions, drain, rinse and put in a bowl.

3. Heat up a pan over medium heat, add milk and bring to a simmer.

4. Add oregano and garlic, stir, remove heat and simmer for 5 minutes.

5. Take off heat and leave aside for 4 minutes.

6. Transfer this to your food processor, mix with cheese, salt and pepper to the taste, parsley and half the avocado and blend well.

7. Transfer pasta to a pot, add blended mix, the rest of the avocado, the bell pepper and the tuna, toss to coat and transfer to a baking dish after you've sprayed it with some cooking oil.

8. In a bowl, mix bread crumbs with paprika, garlic powder and olive oil and stir well.

9. Spread this over casserole, introduce in the oven at 400 degrees F and bake for 15 minutes.

10. Take casserole out of the oven, leave aside to cool down, cut, transfer to plates and serve.

Enjoy!

About the Author

Heston Brown is an accomplished chef and successful e-book author from Palo Alto California. After studying cooking at The New England Culinary Institute, Heston stopped briefly in Chicago where he was offered head chef at some of the city's most prestigious restaurants. Brown decide that he missed the rolling hills and sunny weather of California and moved back to his home state to open up his own catering company and give private cooking classes.

Heston lives in California with his beautiful wife of 18 years and his two daughters who also have aspirations to follow in their father's footsteps and pursue careers in the culinary arts. Brown is well known for his delicious fish and chicken dishes and teaches these recipes as well as many others to his students.

When Heston gave up his successful chef position in Chicago and moved back to California, a friend suggested he use the internet to share his recipes with the world and so he did! To date, Heston Brown has written over 1000 e-books that contain recipes, cooking tips, business strategies for catering companies and a self-help book he wrote from personal experience.

He claims his wife has been his inspiration throughout many of his endeavours and continues to be his partner in business as well as life. His greatest joy is having all three women in his life in the kitchen with him cooking their favourite meal while his favourite jazz music plays in the background.

Author's Afterthoughts

Thank you to all the readers who invested time and money into my book! I cherish every one of you and hope you took the same pleasure in reading it as I did in writing it.

Out of all of the books out there, you chose mine and for that I am truly grateful. It makes the effort worth it when I know my readers are enjoying my work from beginning to end.

Please take a few minutes to write an Amazon review so that others can benefit from your opinions and insight. Your review will help countless other readers make an informed choice

Thank you so much,

Heston Brown

Made in the USA
Las Vegas, NV
02 October 2021